Soul Speaking

Jamila Mikhail

Keep Your Good Heart

Ottawa, Canada

Copyright © 2023 Jamila Mikhail

ISBN 978-1-7753089-4-2

All rights reserved. No part of this publication may be reproduced, distributed, or transmitted in any form or by any means, including photocopying, recording, or other electronic or mechanical methods, without the prior written permission of the author, except in the case of brief quotations embodied in critical reviews and certain other noncommercial uses permitted by copyright law.

Visit www.jamilamikhail.com for contact information or write to jamilamikhail@email.com for inquires.

This is a work of fiction. Names, characters, businesses, places, events and incidents are either the products of the author's imagination or used in a fictitious manner. Any resemblance to actual persons, living or dead, or actual events is purely coincidental.

Cover image available under a CC0 1.0 Universal Public Domain Dedication license <https://creativecommons.org/publicdomain/zero/1.0/>. Used with permission.

To Duane,

The fakest and most hypocritical pathetic excuse of a friend I've ever had. I wouldn't wanna be you when people know what most of this book is about.

These words come from the bottom of my soul. Revenge is a dish best served cold.

Acknowledgements

Since this is primarily a book of hurt and hate (but also of breaking free from toxic people and healing), there are not many people to thank. I'm not going to thank the people who inspired the dark poems you're about to read but I do wish to thank my mom, my cats, my dear friend Christy and my University of Ottawa professors for having been good to me since I published my last book four years ago. Thank you to Carl Martens for lending his voice to the stunning audiobook version of this book as well.

I also thank my readers who have been around since my very first poetry book came out in 2018. None of my books would have been possible without you, your continued support and your good reviews. I hope that this book will have been worth the wait.

Lastly, I will not forget my fellow writers who participated in NaNoWriMo 2022, which is when most of this book came to life and was put together, and kept me accountable.

Content Warning

This book is intended for mature audiences. It contains mentions of abuse, violence, death and other sensitive material that may be upsetting to some readers.

Towards Eternity

One day
The shadows will surround me
Envelope me
Like a blanket
Underneath a sea of stars
Looking down on me

Forgetting
The wrongs and the rights
I'll face the truth
The darkness
And the light
One last time

I'll accept things
As they are
Leave the past behind me
Walk forth
Head held high
Towards eternity

Eight Years

Eight years
Of my life wasted
Eight years
Of my life that you took away
Eight years
For them, I want you to pay

I was just eighteen
When you took advantage of me
Tied an albatross around my neck
Showed me absolutely no respect
You punched me in the gut
After eight years I've had enough

Eight years
I stood by you
Eight years
Of shit you put me through
Eight years
For me to hate you

I can breathe now that you're gone
After all the times you've done me wrong
You can rot exactly where you are
Alone with a darkened heart
You're rotten to the core
This should've ended long before

Eight years
You took everything
Eight years
I gave you anything
Eight years
All of it for nothing

I'm moving on with my life
Sometimes there's goodness in goodbye
There are no tears on my behalf
I've given you the final slap
Go ahead and abuse someone else
Because you'll never touch me again

Moving On

Now that night has fallen
And the cold air is coming in
I think of what you put me through
And I'm glad you're gone

You walking away
Was the best thing you could do for me
I'm thankful that you're gone
Even if the pain still lingers on

But I won't let this build up
Inside of me
I'll probably never forgive you
But I gladly let you go

I don't hold on to you
Your lies, your hypocrisy
Your betrayals or your toxicity
You're dead to me

I'm moving on
Still standing, still strong
So goodbye, good riddance
Thanks for the ride, but I'm gone

Letter of Apology

Dear Toni Michelle
You don't know me
And you'll never read this
But I'm writing to you today
To say I'm sorry

I'm sorry that I didn't believe you
That I believed your abuser instead
Time and experience
Have made me see and understand
What was previously obscure to me

Please remember
That I was very young too
Oblivious to the evils in the world
But they revealed themselves to me
Like they did to you

I see now that it wasn't love
And it never was
I haven't been in your shoes
So I apologize for my ignorance
And not taking your side

I hope you've put this behind you
And are living a fulfilling life
I'm struggling to move on myself
But things are better this way

Now that he's out of both our lives

I can see clearly now
After having been blind for so long
After having believed his lies
And his stories
In which he's always the victim

I should have defended you
Instead I believed him
Until he deceived me too
He took everything that was good
And then threw me away

So I hope you can forgive me
This hasn't been easy on me
But I'm grateful for the lesson
That this experience has taught me
As I walk forth with peace

Love of a Soldier

I look into his eyes
Before one last goodbye
Another kiss on the lips
And that's it

Now you're leaving
You're leaving
I won't see you for a year
I don't even know if you'll come back here

One year in Iraq
And I'm not sure you'll come back
No matter how many times I wish you luck
I still miss you so much

Everyday I think about you
And I'm sure you think about me too
I fell in love with a deploying soldier
After you go there will be no other

Will I ever see you again?
Will you come home in the end?
Everyday I live in uncertainty
Despite that you tell me not to worry

Will I have to carry your coffin?
To the cemetery, to be buried and forgotten
You'll be one of the many

But you'll always be a part of me

I will always remember you
No matter what the world puts me through
You are my hero
And I will always love you so

Gone

Here I surprise myself again
Not being as sad as I should be
Considering that you're gone
I'm happy you're no longer around

You truly, deeply hurt me
Your arrogance and your hypocrisy
Disguised as love
But given as abuse

Despite the pain I can breathe again
Free from the hold you had on me
For nearly a decade
I was in the palm of your hand

But today I'm glad you're gone
Sitting in prison until your old age
Alone with your regrets and your sins
You're exactly where you belong

Write

Write when you're happy
Write when you're sad
Write when you're good
Write when you're bad

Write to take the pain away
Write so you can feel
Write to get carried away
Write so you can heal

Write when you're mad
Write when you cry
Write on the best day of your life
Write when everything's gone awry

Writing is screaming in silence
No matter what you're shouting
Write no matter what is happening
It'll save you from drowning

They say sharing is caring
So write down the words
Even if they don't mean anything
Because they really mean the world

New Beginning Haiku

A new beginning
The freedom envelopes me
A good life awaits

Parliament Hill

In my daydream
I stand in the breeze
The flags unable to be still
Behind me on Parliament Hill

The sun shines bright
With the promise of a new life
A dawning of a miracle
There at Parliament Hill

Our eyes sparkle with joy
Two heartbeats drown out the noise
Agape flowed, curing our ills
Upon our first meeting on Parliament Hill

The Secret

I have never seen your face
Is it really a piece of such disgrace?
I've only seen you from behind
What is this secret you try to hide?
The secrets that you hide seem more like lies
Lies being covered up
Such as this
Keeping your mouth shut
Because so many things just don't work out
When you're not around
We don't seem to click like we used to
And it's driving us further apart
It hurts me in the heart
Roses are red, violets are blue
I did my best at loving you
This filthy little secret
Do you trust me enough to keep it?
Your life is a beautiful denial
On which you shall stand trial
Behind your beautiful eyes
Tell me
What is this secret you try to hide?

Speak

The winds of uncertainty blow
As the seeds of hatred grow
Widows line up in the roads
Holding caskets, row upon row

Remember what happened in 1933?
Why are you so quick to forget history?
And quickly disregard such tyranny?
Are your eyes not open to see?

Try to make us believe that socialism kills
While you're dropping bombs for a thrill
We will resist, you can bet the hell we will
We'll resist all the way to Capitol Hill

Oppression, war, rape and bloodshed
Is that how you make America great again?
Bloodthirsty zealots like you fill us with dread
Because the last one left 60 million dead

The innocent pay the heaviest price
Through the darkness, chase the light
Having to fight another day just to survive
A never-ending battle to live and let die

You might silence us, that's true
You never protected the communist or the Jew
But you can expect your own downfall too

Then, who will you expect to speak for you?

Favourite Penpal

Be it by chance, or by pure happenstance
Life made it so that we would cross paths
It may seem like we are worlds apart
But the distance is mended by letters and cards

You truly are like no other
I think of you as my brother
The one I was never lucky enough to have
But apparently fate had other plans

We aren't where we want to be in life
But it's easier with someone by your side
No matter what happens, why or where
Just think of me and I'll be there

Seventeen

Seventeen crosses up on a hill
Life lost like a winter's chill
Part of me died that day
That's all I can really say
So what happened?
What went wrong?
What could I have done differently?
Now it's too late, apparently
I can't go back
Can't undo what is done
It's too late
I failed
The clouds and their somber stare
Look down on you in despair
Their frozen tears of sorrow
Land where young lives used to bloom
How could you do something like this?
When your life was just about to begin
You ended it all so tragically
You were just seventeen

Outer Space

I am the great unknown
One more lost soul
No other reason left to be
No other reason left to see
Somewhere there's a parallel universe
That's looking back at me
Somewhere in outer space
I won't be so lonely

I Hate

I hate it when you're here
I hate it when you're gone
I hate the way I need you when you're not around
I hate the way I need you and don't know where you are

I hate it when you say you love me
I hate it because I know you don't really mean it
I hate it when you say you'll always be there for me
I hate it because we both know you're not

I hate that I love you
I hate that I do
I hate that no matter what I can't hate you
I hate the way you comfort me

I hate the way it never lasts
I hate the things you say to me
I hate the way I can't help but believe them
I hate the way you hurt me

I hate the way I hurt myself
I hate the way the blame always ends up on me
I hate the things you do to me
I hate the happiness that comes with them

I hate missing you
I hate it when you ignore me
I hate that I can't tell you how I feel

I hate that you have better things to do

I hate that I'm your last priority
I hate that I feel this way
I hate that I have to live like this
I hate that I'll have to replace you

I hate making decisions because you can't step up
I hate the way you make me smile
I hate the way you always help me when I'm in denial
I hate that you then have to go away

I hate that I have to miss you
I hate that I have to love you
I hate that it feels like you were never here
I just hate everything

I just hate it all

Levi

Can it be true, oh Levi?
That you think about me too?
The same way I think about you
When you don't sleep at night

Sometimes you're the reason I cry
Do you know this, oh Levi?
It's my fault, that's partially true
Because I'm the one who left you

I stood by your side through high tides
But in my time of need you weren't there
Oh Levi, is that how you show you care?
Those tides swept us both aside

I hope you find happiness and start anew
Away from your lies, I will with someone else
Oh Levi, just admit it to yourself
You left me long before I left you

The End of the Journey

Hearing your voice is more than a dream
It's more than just sublime
I remember when I saw you for the first time
I remember when you said goodbye for the last time

I wish you hadn't left so fast
I always thought that this would last

Your existence reminds me daily
That everything in this life is temporary
But over time my memory has faded
The hands of time haven't left me jaded

I hope you enjoy the next part of your journey
While I'm holding on to your memory

I still think of you from time to time
Once in a while you still pop up in my mind
I wonder if you think of me too
Like I sometimes think about you?

We'll probably never see each other again
But it was nice knowing you in the end

Old Friends

Hey there my friend
It's been a while
How have you been?

I haven't seen you in ages
I haven't gotten your letters
Nothing but blank pages

I used to miss you a lot
But time has since passed
And I've almost forgotten you

Call me sometime
I'd be happy to hear your voice
Even after all this time has gone

I'd love for things to be like before
For us to pick up where we left off
So just reach out to me

You know it's true
That we had good times together
So let's get together again

Catch up on how things have been
Get to know each other again
And see where we go from here

A Tomorrow Without You

I expect to see you tomorrow
Will you come to see me?
I can't wait for you
Can't wait any longer
I'm growing weaker
Without you

I'm not satisfied knowing
That you've forgotten about me
I don't want to wait for you
Not for a moment longer
Even if it's the death of me
I want to be free

For my own sake
Don't come by tomorrow
Stop holding me down
I want my strength back
But I know I'll disintegrate
Without you

From Life To Death

My bones tremble
My heart beats faster
I cannot breathe
I feel my temperature rise

A crime of fate
The breath of life
Like hands around my neck
There's nothing I can do

Collapse to the floor
Everything you thought you knew
Life is slipping away
You are no more

My heart falls to pieces
I'm out of breath
My eyes fill with water
The struggle is over

Dust to dust
Ashes to ashes
From life to death
I will not forget

The Knight and the Princess

Now I'm laying down to sleep
Hoping that you're in my dreams
Where I'm a knight full of power
Going to free you from the enchanted tower
Are you a princess being saved by a knightly brother?
Or is the knight a long-distance lover?
It's a wonderful story we both could weave
Since we are prisoners in a harsh reality
It's through the stories we write
That we are able to live full lives
Your letters are bringers of honey
You're the sunflower that shines for me
Perhaps sometime in the future
It's you who'll be my rescuer

Winter Snowfall

Winter snow is falling
On the outside world today
Through the window it's calling
For me to come out and play

Not long ago I could have gone
Bundled up for warmth and carefree
To jump in the snow covering the lawn
Prior to this wheelchair carrying my body

But the snow is different now
Because my body is locked away
But I can still smile instead of frown
When it melts, deciding not to stay

The End of a Friendship

Why have you betrayed me?
I know what you've been saying
It took a true friend to help me see
That a fool is what I've been playing

I understand completely now
You wholeheartedly deceived me
But how could that be?
Now I can actually see
Who is the real enemy

Luckily I have allies
People who truly care
One is effectively a spy
Who gave me the facts, taking a dare
Explained the extent of your lies
And that you were not playing fair

I told you my deepest secret
But somehow your friends all know
Why couldn't you keep it?
That truly was the lowest blow

You told others vile things about me
Yet I always respected you
And you said you never even liked me
You must think I'm a monkey in a zoo

I must say that I'm not pleased
I'm more like a lion, that part is true
You're making a powerful enemy
Saying you're sorry just won't do

Don't try to explain
You've already done that before
Just read this final complaint
Because you won't hear from me anymore

The Attack

So you want to play games
Well, let's begin this charade
You've already dealt the first blows
I must admit they were pretty low
Now that the fight in me is back
Prepare yourself to be attacked
I can still strike with all my might
You will never win this fight
My attack will not be physical
But with words that make it mental
It was with words that you first struck
But now you're running out of luck
I know how you truly feel
I'm an enemy from whom you'll never heal
You've ruthlessly ripped out my heart
And literally tore it all apart
But my mind did not crack
This is me bouncing back
Using words to hurt me was unwise
Because these same words will be your demise

Once Loved

It makes me sad to see you like this
It angers me that you have to do this to yourself
I'm sick and tired of having to watch you pass in front of the house
Almost unable to walk a straight line

All I seem to see are the scars on your arms
And the marks around your neck
Your discoloured lips
Your pale white skin

It kills me to see you do this
I don't want to attend your funeral
But it seems like I'll be holding your little hand in your coffin soon
Tears come down my cheeks every time I think of you

I've seen the miracles you could make
And now all I can see is all the pain you have to take
It makes me sick to see you like this
Your smile used to tell me that you were doing so well

Now the track marks on your arms have another story to tell
I used to see your eyes shine in the sunlight
Now you never leave the darkness
How could you go back to this?

Destiny was calling your name
You had the whole world at your feet, waiting for you
Now you're back to chasing delusions with fishing nets
You're so close to breathing your last breath

I can't seem to let you go but our friendship was
something I won't soon forget
You were great
Pleasant to be around
I hope the ones on the other side take you into their
arms

And give you all the love you could ever have beyond this
world
I'm sad to see that you have to end like this
But I guess now there's nothing more I can say
Because I don't know when it's going to be your last day

But until then I'll make sure to tell the girl on the other
side of the mirror
That I once loved her

Dear Pen Friend

I've racked my brain several ways
And continue to draw a blank
As to what words to say
So far, the ideas have all sank

You came into my life
As a star in the deep of night
I was going through some strife
When you brought a glimmer of light

Your letters always bring a smile
Even before they're read
I can make no denial
That you keep my heart from death

You've given me cause to aspire
Keeping my heart open as you see
You're a friend I admire
Taking interest in all of my deeds

Sometimes I can be lazy
And as a human I fail
But it does drive me crazy
That we correspond at the pace of a snail

Time isn't taken into account
Since we both show patience as well
Letters are written, there's no doubt

But in the meantime, I can't help but dwell

So my dear pen friend, thank you
For all the kindness you have shown
Our bonds of friendship proved true
As long as the sands of time will blow

Nature's Song

I walk about in a different world
While around me reality swirls
No one else is able to see
The sky, the rivers, or forests of trees
I'm the only one who hears
The howl of the wolves from far and near
That's the reality in which I belong
Able to listen to nature's song
The howl of the wolf, the coyote's yap
Is a song to which I could easily take a nap
I remember their music daily in my mind
It's something that helps me to survive
When I'm discouraged to the point of tears
The wolf's howl drives away my fears
Now if my enemies could only see
The wolf that also lives inside of me

In Pursuit of the Storm

I'm listening to music when a weather alert cuts in
The meteorologist says tornadoes have begun to spin
Joining the chase is my desire from within
But the fear makes the sweat roll down my skin

I hear the sound of thunder, wind and rain
Making music that goes deep into my brain
But tonight there's no sound like a train
Because the storm above me is tame

I let my imagination run free
While they talk about flying debris
My heart recalls the past with glee
When tornadoes didn't scare me

Maybe one day I'll return to chasing storms as a pursuit
But for the moment the skies have left me destitute
A consequence of life bearing me bad fruit
I've slammed the door to the weather, giving it the boot

One day I'll get up and be confined no more
I'll walk through that now securely locked door
I'll chase storms that now are only lore
But in the meantime my spirit can still soar

Forever Friend

You've had my back many times
Been my friend through thick and thin
Even I missed the signs
Being involved in something I couldn't win

You didn't abandon me
You answered the call
So alone, I wouldn't be
As I continued to fall

My friend forever no matter the cost
It really should have been much more
If only ourselves we hadn't lost
Our hearts together could have soared

What's done is done, the past is the past
And the future is in a state of flux
Tying you down in the way that you've asked
I'm afraid would only make things more rough

Calling All Scumbags

Sitting in my dark place alone
I wonder what went wrong
No one seems to know
The reason you have no soul

Stick a knife right through your throat
And let someone else take oath
Just to make sure you can get there first
For whatever that to you it's worth

Calling all scumbags
Broken promises and filthy little lies
Let the fire ignite in your eyes
And your sick twisted smile

I'm calling all scumbags

You took the breath straight out of me
And left a whole where my heart ought to be
I'm sick and tired of being angry
I want you to drown in my misery

Sadness and hate
Two emotions you can't replace
I just wish I could slap you in the face
For all the times you left without a trace

Calling all scumbags

Broken promises and filthy little lies
Let the fire ignite in your eyes
And your sick twisted smile

I'm calling all scumbags

Too cowardly to admit it
You worthless piece of shit
Go and slit your wrist
You're one scumbag I will not miss

Now it's all been made very clear
That I don't need or want you here
And in this world that surrounds me
I'm overjoyed you disappeared

Calling all scumbags
Broken promises and filthy little lies
Let the fire ignite in your eyes
And your sick twisted smile

I'm calling all scumbags

Remorse should have shown
But oh no, your heart is made of stone
Beneath my teeth hear the groan
You can die and rot alone

Let the salt enter the wound
Your end is coming soon
You don't know what I can do

No you don't have a clue

Calling all scumbags
Broken promises and filthy little lies
Let the fire ignite in your eyes
And your sick twisted smile

I'm calling all scumbags

Now don't try to hide
Now that the world is mine
When everything you are falls behind
I want you to choke when you swallow your pride

Light the fire and walk away
One day you will pay
Until then don't make the pain go away
No you scumbag, make it stay

Calling all scumbags
Broken promises and filthy little lies
Let the fire ignite in your eyes
And your sick twisted smile

I'm calling all scumbags

This time you won't be heard
You greedy little bastard
You will get what you deserve
You greedy little bastard
You will get what you deserve

My Share

If I could speak to you
I'd have a lot to say
The eyes I used to love
Are no longer sparkling blue
Results of this environment
And the storms that passed through
There was sometimes
Seldom reasons to smile
Especially through the many trials
There are questions I would ask
If it wasn't a forbidden task
I'd ask you why you did this
If things really ended how you wished
How was any of this deserved?
Was this my share of the dessert?
Revenge is a dish best served cold
Both for the young and the old
Ill will I do not bear
But you won't be in my prayers

Cafeteria Food

To the cafeteria building
I am heading
It's a catastrophe
That I am dreading
Because in the cafeteria
I will be eating
And when the road kill sets in
For my life I will be pleading

Rollercoaster

Twisting and turning
And downward spiralling
This rollercoaster isn't real exciting
The day I got on, it seemed real inviting
But then it began its downhill driving
Now my emotions are extremely confusing
My life they are completely ruining
This is causing too much hurting
But I have no strength left for fighting
The only logical course is retreating
So inward I am turning
My emotions never outwardly revealing
And my thoughts not disclosing
In my bubble I'm hiding
Into myself I am withdrawing

Victim Haiku

I was your victim
But now I'm a survivor
At last free from you

Murderous Poem

The only thing that would make today any worse
Would be driving away in a hearse
My anger boils deep inside my veins
How do I get it out without causing pain?

Inside my basement I will hide
To make up this mind of mine
On whether I should put a bullet in my gun
Or just forget about this and run

My inner demons I shall seek
So my mind can have peace
At last you will be gone forever
And I shall sleep much, much better

Beside my bed my shotgun I will keep
So I'm safe at night when I sleep
And if my house, I find you inside
The coroner's van will be your next ride

Battleship

You attempted to sink my boat
But you didn't know how well it could float
No matter the stormy seas you brought to my life
Not only did I survive, but now you can watch me thrive

I haven't missed you once since you've been gone
Now that I sail alone the seas are calm
The only thing you ever did was weigh me down
But I'm the one who smiled as you drowned

These words come from the innermost depths of my soul
My friend, revenge is a dish best served cold
So go ahead and do what you do
Because my life is a million times better without you

Left To Drown

We're not anything alike anymore
In fact, I don't even know who you are
I have no idea how things came to that
But I know I don't want you back
You don't get to control everything anymore
Never again, not like before
You've said what you wanted to say
Now I've moved on, so go away
If you won't leave then listen to me
I'm better off without you as you'll see
You can shove your cowboy hat
As far as it'll go up your ass
There's nothing you can do to bring me back
I'm way passed that
So what are you gonna do now?
Now that you're alone, left to drown

How I Really Feel

I want to tell you that I love you
But these are words I cannot say
Because you said you loved another
And I'd just be in the way

I filled the week with activity
And a list of social events
To keep my feelings for you from surfacing
But it's something I couldn't prevent

I want to be with you forever
That's what you'd told me before
Now you see me as your sibling
I can't take the confusion anymore

You stole my heart and tore it in two
It really was a hard blow
But since I don't want to hurt you
I can never let you know

Start Anew

I'm torn between two worlds
Of darkness and of light
Around me all things swirl
Revealing creatures of the night

Agony, despair and sadness
Is found everywhere I roam
There is no more gladness
Knowing you'll be alone

I've been the angel by your side
Your fiercest defender
A ray of hope and light
I know you'll always remember

I've given my all and tried my best
I've helped you through many nights
Now it comes down to your biggest test
Will you give up or continue to fight?

I'll never give up fighting for you
I won't allow the darkness to win
You aren't theirs anymore, that's the truth
It's time for your battle in this to end

I've given you the keys
You know what to do
Now I'm begging you please

Let it all go and start anew

Insanity

Insanity
Crawling into me
Into my head
I'm wishing I was dead
Thoughts fill my brain
Driving me insane
Ideas of suicide
And ways to die
Corrupting my mind
I'm going insane
I can't set things straight

Winds of Change

The questions grow in my mind
Do you dream of me?
The answer, I fear to find
Knowing it may bring me grief

Because now I know what you are
And your face haunts me
You left me with nothing but scars
In this darkness where I cannot see

Your true colours have definitely shown
What you did fills me with anger
Thankfully a wind of change has blown
And I'm no longer under your finger

You deserve all the grief you get
And you are where you belong
Because I'll never be able to forget
But I don't miss you now that you're gone

You can ask Satan to spare your soul
And perish in an abyss without light
You don't deserve to be in this world
You know you lost this fight

The Foggy Mirror

Who are you?
And why are you here?
Those two questions
Have no answers, I fear

The foggy face in the mirror
Is unknown to me
Even if it were made clearer
Myself, I still wouldn't see

Who am I? I don't know
These circumstances hide
The side of me I used to show
And who I really am inside

The portrait this situation paints
Is filled only with deceit
And shows a person willed with taint
Obscuring the real me

Final Letter

I'd prayed for a fresh start
And a way to begin anew
As you continuously broke my heart
Through and through

I didn't bargain on everything being lost
I forgot that words have a lot of power
That reminder came at a great cost
As my world was progressively devoured

Looking back, now I can see
Your words and promises never meant much
Your destruction is what finally set me free
Of you constantly breaking my trust

That you'd always stand by my side
Came wherever I went
Was just another one of your lies
Another promise you never meant

Your own hand has now done the thing
Against which you begged and pleaded
Your cries still make my ears ring
Even though I gave in, I conceded

I can't explain the relief
And my complete lack of surprise
When your final letter reached me

Revealing all of your hypocrisies

So with my blessing you may go
Because you were never true
Enjoy your bitch from long ago
Until she sees your true colours too

Oklahoma City

If I could go back
What changes would I make?
If my options did not lack
And my future I could retake

Would I go back to high school?
And to my first love?
When I knew all the rules
And everything was peaceful like a dove

Would I go back to my college days?
When I was more carefree?
And when things didn't go my way
I found a good friend to help me

Would I go back to Oklahoma City?
To a time where there was no strife
And decide it was the place to be
Forever changing my life

Two things I'd surely change
To avoid this mental prison I'm in
I'd never wander and leave my home range
Or allow any of this shit to begin

I would have let you end your own life
I would refuse to save you
I would not have helped you fight

Because in the end you killed me too

Shackles of Love

So many thoughts keep spinning around my head
The good, the bad and the unknown
This loneliness and this desolation
Is the equivalent of sitting in my head all alone

Sometimes I wish that you could just leave
Just leave and leave me alone
Other times I'd sew our souls together

All that is left of you now are the scars on my heart
I swear I will tear it all apart
I carved your name into my arm
Promising you that I would never do you any harm

I carved your name into my soul
Promising you that I would never let you go
But you're the one that let go
You were the only good in me

Now living with myself is all I have
Do you know what it's like?
To look at yourself, paralyzed?
This soul is just no good

So I can beg you to save me for all that I am
Or beg you to save me for the fuck of it
I know my life will end
But I won't give this life away again

You broke my trust, shattered my existence

So lift up my sleeves and see the pattern of my cuts
My flesh is all I have
This life is not enough
You think you're so clever or whatever
I'm done with your endeavours

I'm needing no one's help
I'm needing only you
Sometimes I can still feel your presence

It still lingers here
Some days I get so lonely
That the loneliness won't leave me alone
Sometimes it hurts so bad that I can't breathe
I can only tell myself that you still love me

But I don't believe my own lies
Like I believed yours
Don't you miss the way we were?
We promised one another that we'd love each other forever

Forever didn't last very long
I guess that in the end it didn't really matter
It didn't even matter no matter how hard I tried
You slipped away, and I don't know why

Every time I try to live without you I feel dead
But I can't breathe when I'm with you

So what are we really doing here?
You hesitated
And now I wish that you would just go away

Just leave me here forever in the dark
Was this love just a waste of time?
I guess you'll never get to see my face again
All the miracles you traced

I can't explain what it's like
To wonder if I'll ever cross your mind
I loved you so much it hurt
For whatever it was worth

This can't be heaven, it feels like I'm hell
Looking out the window into the blowing snow
I never thought that hell could be so cold

Just another helpless plea, I beg you
I will love you forever
The end
Just don't leave me here again

I've seen the world change
And watch it go back from where it came
I guess I was just an alternative
Just another option until the past came back
Now I'm in second place for a second chance

I'm tired of chasing delusions
All I need is someone to believe in

You brought me back to life
Only to let me die

They say that the higher you are, the farther you fall
You seemed too good to be true
And I guess you were too

But why pull me up and then tear me down?
I gave you all I had
I gave you all I had to give
I guess I did it all for nothing because now that you're gone away
You didn't even say goodbye to me
Hope is lost
Now all I can do is drown away in my own misery

I keep telling myself that one day you will burn
That one day you will get what you deserve
Some people never learn
Sometimes I just want to make you hurt
Like the way I hurt
I know it's messed up but it makes me feel better

Sometimes I wish I had never ever met you at all
But all I can say now is
Don't put your life in someone's hands that's bound to steal it away
We were supposed to burn the world together
But you were the fire
And I'm the one who burned
All I've ever said was the truth

And yes I really loved you
You must not forget that I hurt too
You said such sweet words
Unlike anything I had ever heard

But I guess it was just a cover up for corruption and shame
You burned down my perfect little world
I never thought I was crazy
Until you showed up
I never thought I could love, never thought I could trust

You proved it to me only to prove it to yourself
That you're always better than everyone else
The days could go on forever
And I would still never leave your side
Nothing you could do could ever bring me back to life
So save your last goodbyes

I used to feel so loved
Now I'm just screwed up
You shouldn't blame yourself because I guess I deserved it
Although I never thought I'd believe it
These millions of memories make up my millions of shattered dreams

I guess that even the brightest light will fade away to black
I guess my love just wasn't enough
Forgive me if I do not understand

One day we'll be lying in the earth
Side by side
But until the end there's only one thing you should know
I'll love you until the end of days

Domestic Disturbance

Nowhere else to go
Nowhere left to turn
It's been so many years
And you have yet to learn

What's to show for it all?
You constantly asking, what about me?
Problems not ceasing, actions unchanging
Facebook on the phone, Mario on the Wii

Of the many mounds of laundry
Not a single load gets done
As for clean dishes
In this house there are none

There's no one left to help
And you obviously don't care
All those bridges have burned
And I'm running out of prayers

What will it take?
Why can't you see?
The problem here is
Your lack of responsibility

To you it's all one big game
I hope it's fun while it lasts
It's gotten rather lame

You leaving me no time to relax

Spiritual Battle

I see with eyes unclouded
The secret that you bear
You searched to confide but doubt
Fearing your secret would be shared

One fateful night
It all made sense
I saw you in a new light
And came to your defence

As we talked and shared
And to a realization we came
It caught us both unprepared
To learn our secrets are the same

I've been close to where you are now
Although it's not exactly the same
You've gone further down
And are on a darker plane

The problem is not physical
And is not winnable in our realm
This fight is spiritual
And started in the depths of Hell

There are warriors of prayer
Requesting angels of light
To reach you in your darkest hour

And make sure you're alright

The warriors of darkness are defeated
They have nothing on which to stand
For you the angels have interceded
You only need to take their hand

Let It Go

I'm torn between two worlds
Of darkness and of light
Around me all things swirl
Revealing creatures of the night

Agony, despair and sadness
No matter where I roam
It's hard to find the gladness
In this broken home

Leave the past where it is
It's all been said before
Let it go, that's my wish
And don't bring it up no more

Just let things go
Just let it be
I've run out of rope
Dealing with your jealousy

If there is still hope
There can still be peace
Just let it all go
Don't hold on, just release

Prayer

How is it that I'm still torn?
Between the darkness and the light
Insanity could become the norm
If I were to give up the fight

To the darkness I could call
Forsaking all I know
Choosing again to fall
By embracing powers from below

I hear the whispers every single day
In thoughts and dreams that don't cease
Saying it doesn't have to be this way
That darkness could provide my release

The darkness wants me to be a slave
I know the truth extremely well
And I don't want it to be this way
I refuse to embark on a train to hell

My God, please hear my prayer
I feel so isolated and alone
Save me from all this despair
Have mercy and bring me home

Until the End of Time

I'll be long gone and rotting in hell
Before you say I love you to someone else
I promised I'd love you until my death
And even after than I won't be done yet

So if you die before I do
Somebody better tell the coroner he'll have two
Around my neck I'll wear a hangman's noose
Because I never want to be away from you

The moment I saw your pretty face
I knew it was you and no one else
In that same moment we sealed our fate
I promised to never leave you by yourself

So boy you better never tell me goodbye
Because I won't leave you even when I die
I want to have your body buried next to mine
I want to be with you until the end of time

Owed Apology

You owe me an apology
But it's too late to say you're sorry
You're not the same person you were before
You're not that person anymore

You used your religion against me
And to hide your hypocrisy
But eventually the mask falls away
And I see you in the light of day

Sometimes I miss the way it used to be
But I thank God you can no longer abuse me
The sun will eventually shine again
Even if I may not exactly know when

At the end of the day
I'm glad that you've gone away
So you can shove your apology up your ass
Because I'm never taking you back

Calling All Angels

Do you call my name?
I can't hear your voice
I'm not the one to blame for this mess
You're all I have left

Calling all angels
Please come take me away
I'm no longer strong enough
To face the days

Put an end to this tragic play
That my life has come to portray
Have mercy on my soul
And save me from this world

Please take me by the hand
The people down here don't understand
This prayer is from the bottom of my soul
From inside my being as a whole

Practicing (Original Version)

To the music building I am flying
It's actually very exciting
Because my trumpet I will be practicing
So I can say I did when I find someone asking
My musical skills I will be testing
For a concert where I will not be resting
Because when I do my best performing
My attitude is never storming

Practicing (Alternate Version)

To the music building I am flying
It's actually a bit exciting
On my trumpet I hope I'll be playing
Asking, I'll say yes and not be lying
Yes I practiced, I won't be stopping
Concert's coming soon, I can't be resting
I prefer to do my best at performing
So I won't be caught unhappy, frowning

Promise Haiku

If it takes forever
I'll find you no matter what
The ends of the earth

Say Goodnight

Sitting alone in my dimly lit room
My thoughts race back to you
I'm burned out, completely spent
Spiritually, mentally, physically, emotionally
Because of what you did to me

Give me a hundred reasons to stay
I'll give you a hundred reasons to leave
There's nothing you could ever say
That would convince me otherwise
You took away my identity

My innocence was lost
I desperately plead for you to stop hurting me
I don't believe any of your excuses anymore
So just save your breath
And say goodnight

Turning Point

What can I say but that I didn't see
All I know is that you mean so much to me
I had to somewhat read between the lines
I must have missed that the first time

You told me that I misunderstood
But I didn't see how I could
You said one thing then another
You loved me forever, but then no longer

I was very confused
My heart was extremely bruised
A deep sadness set in
And I lost my will to win

I buried my feelings deep inside
Formed a bubble around myself to hide
Because I didn't want anyone to see
My pain and my misery

But then I made a mistake
You read it and it was too late
I didn't really want you to know
How you had hurt me so

But today I started my way back up
It happened on a stroke of luck
I talked to a very dear friend

On whom I could depend

I told you my story just today
You promised that you would pray
I didn't know what else to say
So I turned away

You had to leave so I said goodbye
Walked away with my spirit rising to the sky
A spark of hope was lit inside
Now there's more I'd like to ignite

There was another who helped me today
He doesn't know it yet so I won't say
He is someone who doesn't know me well
But that will change soon I can tell

Wuthering Heights

I remember the stars in the sky
They were so bright
So shiny that night
Just like the sparkle in your eyes

It must've been the heat of the moment
Because I felt like I'd been hit by lightning
Yet the love was already so deep
Deeper than the deepest depths of the sea

I knew from the start I couldn't keep you
But I'd still enjoy you
For however long I had you
For however many days God gave you

What was once romantic turned to tragedy
When you were taken away from me
Every night I pray your ghost haunts me
So I wouldn't be here so lonely

I cannot live without my life
I cannot live without my soul
When your memory comes back to me
I'm taken right back to Wuthering Heights

My world may have stopped turning
As long as my heart remains in mourning
But I have the promise of seeing you again

Still together, as we remain

I wish we could've had a different ending
Perhaps we will in another life
Just like Cathy and Heathcliff
Reunited until the end of time

I Do / I Don't

I don't want this to get worst
I don't
But I've reached the end
The end of my rope

I just don't know where to start
I don't
I've already tried everything
Everything I could think of

I want to make things right
I do
I really don't want to lose you
But I don't know what else to do

I want to be happy
I do
 And I want you by my side
But not the way you are now

I don't know you anymore
I don't
Who have you become?
You only look like who I knew

I don't like you anymore
I don't
Not when you take me for granted

Like I've never been wanted

I wish things could be otherwise
I do
But this is out of my control
Now the ball is in your court

Do you think we'd be better apart?
I do
So maybe goodbye gives us a new start
The second chance we both desire

The Complete Unknown

There's one place that I'll never call my home
And that's the very bottom of your soul
In my life you left an empty hole
I guess there are some things I'll just never know

Who am I to take the blame?
You're the one with all the shame
This is just like a burnt out flame
I guess things will never be the same

I learned the things you never showed me
Became all the things you'd never be
Maybe one day you will see
All this pain and catastrophe

I took the chances you'd have blown
You're the one who left me all alone
So many of our stories will remain untold
And you remain the complete unknown

2012

I want to tell you about 2012
And the events leading up to this hell
There are secrets which I've yet to impart
As they would surely break your heart

Sometimes I don't know how to begin
Other times the events are buried too deep within
I've erected many barriers in my mind
Shielding memories I don't want to find

So perhaps it's best to keep my mouth shut
As myself I don't want to undercut
We should have given each other more respect
Instead of causing this shipwreck

But neither one of us can change the past
Now and forever, as long as it lasts
So perhaps I'll bring my secrets to my grave
And sleep with them in my underground enclave

Remember, it is you who killed me
Yes, I also acknowledge my responsibility
So while you still have me under your spell
Let me tell you about 2012

The Charade

Your friendship is just a charade
Nothing is ever as it seems
To you everything's a game
That causes your eyes to gleam

You and your clever cons, petty tricks
Just seeking whatever you can take
It's a game of which I am sick
Your bullshit is giving me a headache

The crimes continue just the same
No differences do I find
Between the streets that began the game
And the hypocrisy you try to hide

This Madness

Can anyone help me?
Is anyone there?
My world is crashing
Does anyone care?

Twisting and turning
Spiralling down
This path being taken
Is no merry-go-round

Look out, they said
Don't do it, I was warned
But I didn't listen
And now I'm torn

Torn between two worlds
Of darkness and of light
Do I try to stop the madness?
Or do I do what's right?

I don't get it, don't understand
Why can't I see?
It seems like everyone else noticed
What you've been doing to me

Kindness has been tried
But was doomed to fail
Anger is on the opposite side

And only screams and yells

Please, just make it stop
Make it all end
Because before too long
There will be no making amends

Darkness

There's a deep darkness in you
There's no room for any light
Between the two there's the truth
Of each, the opposite is the other side

There's one by day
And the other by night
As conflicted as always
Forever in a fight

An agent of darkness
You ought to call yourself
But you, I'll always resist
That, you should be able to tell

Dear Father

To the man I'm supposed to call my father
To me you're the complete unknown
I guess it's better that you just don't bother
All of the skeletons in the closet will be left alone

I'm the daughter you can't hide
Pray for your life before you pray for mine
I'm just the forgotten child
The one you left behind

So many years were lost, milestones ignored
Since you've been gone without a trace
I'm getting comfortable knowing that
You're just a sperm donor without a face

A father without a son
Is like a bullet without a gun
But what about a father without his daughter?
I guess you can't spell manslaughter without laughter

Did you intend to make it hurt?
To make it all disappear into the dirt?
All the things I had to go through
And it's all because of you

Do you feel any shame?
Because I feel a lot of pain
You cut me and took my breath

This will end how it began

If you're out there somewhere
I don't know if you care
It seems like you don't
So you remain the complete unknown

All we had, gone forever
Things that you said would never be
Living without you doesn't bother me
Yours truly, your daughter

My Favorite Person

You've always seemed so brave
And would so easily smile
Even when things were grey
You radiated happiness, not denial

I can recall no better time
Than those few moments we spent
Looking at the starts in the sky
Before began this lament

You are special and adored
May no one make you believe otherwise
Let your heart dare to soar
And your dreams not be denied

You are loved very much
Secret keeper and best friend
In each other we can always trust
And on each other we can depend

You like my stories and my rhymes
Very often you'd seek advice
I miss you calling anytime
To get a laugh when you'd rather cry

I have another secret to impart
Did you ever guess, could you ever tell?
You hold a key to my heart

Do I hold one to yours as well?

Out of everyone I know, to you alone I say
You are my favorite and the best
I'll love you forever and always
To that everyone can attest

Why Bother?

Is anyone out there?
Does anyone care?
My house is in ruin
And it's extremely unfair

No dishes in the cabinet
No clothes in the dresser
The condition of this house
Has become a real stressor

Rotting food on the counters
Trash on the floor
People have made bets
On when I won't be able to take it anymore

What will it take?
Why can't you see?
Why must all the chores
Be left up to me?

I'm the only person
Trying to make this a home
While at the same time I'm working
I may as well be alone

Eight years have now passed
With nothing for it to show
Which chance will be your last?

Even I do not know

You haven't changed
But you demand it of me
Your freedom has no range
While I've stopped being free

You have no problem backstabbing me at all
In front of my friends and wherever you roam
I can't speak, you're the know-it-all
I'm a stranger in my own home

You can't demand of me one thing
And for yourself do another
Meaninglessness is all you ever bring
So why is it that we even bother?

The Rainbow

It's hard to find the words to say
That I hope you're having a good day
To my friend who seems so far away

You've stood by me through thick and thin
Always brightening my days with your friendship
You truly are a wonderful friend

I could ask for no greater gift
Than what you've given me in friendship
I know that to be more is what you wish

If not for current circumstances
I might have given you a chance
But for now your wish I cannot grant

Make a wish when you see a rainbow
May its beauty give you hope
And ask God for the strength to cope

Please always remember one thing
Remember what we're celebrating
Our friendship will carry us through anything

A Spiritual Fight

Twisting and turning
And twirling around
My existence has become
A spiritual battleground

The demons shrouded in darkness
The angels shrouded in light
Swirl around me
Locked in a fight

The demons will not win
Those agents of Hell
Will try to make me give up my faith
But their plans are futile, they will fail

God, my shield, will prevail
Even though pieces may break apart
I shall not be discouraged
Because God is with me in my heart

Angels, send the demons away
And lock them in a jail
Let them fight amongst themselves
And perish in their cell

Five times a day I pray
Bow down to the Lord
To keep me and everyone safe

From these demons at the door

The Red

There's nothing that's gonna stop me
There's nothing that's gonna stop me
Insanity
Insanity

My blood drips on the floor
It's red
Back where I was before
It's all in my head
Thoughts of suicide
Hiding all the tears I keep inside

Insanity
Insanity
Crawling into me
Into my head
All I see is red
I just wish I was dead
It's all red
It's all red
All I see is red
It's all in my head
Red

The calm
Before the storm
Thoughts
Of suicide

So many ways to die
Forget about me
You don't mean anything to me

Insanity
Insanity
Crawling into me
Into my head
All I see is red
I just wish I was dead
It's all red
It's all red
All I see is red
It's all in my head
Red

You're driving me insane
You're driving me insane
Corrupting my mind
Corrupting my mind
Look inside

It's all red
It's all red
Inside my head
You can't stop me

Look at the red
Coming down my arm
All the scars
All the scars

From when you broke my heart

Insanity
Insanity
Crawling into me
Into my head
All I see is red
I just wish I was dead
It's all red
It's all red
All I see is red
It's all in my head
Red

The red creeping into me
The red
Is all that I see
Give into the red
Give into the red
Give into the red

The Chain

I was anchored to hope with a chain
The chain ran out so I added rope
The rope ran out so I added twine
The twine ran out so I added yarn
The yarn ran out so I added string
The string ran out so I added thread
But the spool is nearly empty

Soon I'll be falling towards eternity
Falling into the darkness of this abyss
Oh Lord, don't allow me to not find you
When I can no longer see the light
I accept my fate that I will fall
My prayer is the chance to get back up
And be allowed to tie my chain again

Moving to Indiana

It couldn't have been easy for you
I know it wasn't for me
To suddenly have to move
And uproot everything

I want you to know I can relate
And yes, I really do care
What better time than today
For me to take time to share

Perhaps we wouldn't've ended up here at all
Had it not been for fate
But we're both in this for the long haul
Have faith and take it day by day

My prayer is that one day soon
You'll receive my envelope
And believe that my words are true
So you can have the strength to cope

Before things get busy and I need to run off
I've got one last thing to say
Make time for yourself and have fun
Maybe you'll grow to love Indiana one day

Unnoticed

How long?
How long do I have to wait?
I just can't imagine my future
Without you in it

But you love another
And I exist only in the shadows
You don't notice how I look at you
When you walk into the room

There's gotta be another way
Just one more time
Just one more day
This can't be the only way

Take the time to give me a chance
Take me by the hand
Take me to the dance
But please don't turn away

You're the one
The one and only
In you I have found true love
I truly have

It's all gonna work out
I know it, it has to
Just wait and see

You'll eventually notice me

One day we'll love each other
Then it'll be all that matters
Until then I'll look forward to the day
Where we don't have to say goodbye

A Poem About You

I remember the nights we threw our cares away
And talking to you when the days were grey
I wish we could go back to that time
When we believed everything would be fine
We always got a rise
Out of watching the shooting stars in the sky
Alas, that was all taken away
And I'm no longer feeling so brave
Every ounce of my joy
Was instantaneously taken away
Now an apology is due
This poem was supposed to be about you

The Visiting Angel

It's hard to find the words to say
That capture the essence of this place
Nor can words capture the emotional strife
Of one who faces a certain demise

The last two hours went by too fast
During this visit from an angel from my past
That showed up out of the blue
Serene, beautiful like a painting too

God heard me when I was scared
And today, answered my prayers
When the world surrounds me like a whirlpool
I can count on you to save me from what's cruel

An Innocent Man's Agony

All these people who are leaving quick
Is enough to make me want to be sick
They'll be free in six months, maybe eight
While I'm left to contemplate my fate

My deepest wish is to go home
Not left in this cold jail to roam
I don't cause trouble, curse or scream
So I'll just wait in my cell patiently

Those who make the most commotion
Seem to go home with the swiftest motion
Many brag and boast about their life of crime
And how they'll get away with it next time

There isn't any difference I can see
Between prison and the streets
The crimes continue just the same
Behind these walls meant to shame

How I wish the jury will see
That this world wasn't meant for me
In this place I'm treated just the same
As the man next to me who might be insane

The system has erased my identity
Nobody in here sees me for me
Will the jury fail to see I don't belong here?

Innocent, my days are filled with fear

My brave face is what I don't conceal
While my spirit, daily is killed
I hope the others don't see the lie
And the fear that lurks deep inside

Some may wonder but they don't ask
About the pain hidden behind the mask
Keeping things veiled is a constant test
Ever since I was wrongfully put under arrest

Let me go, that's my daily plea
Hoping these walls won't ever again see me
But no one listens to the cries
Of an innocent man pleading for his life

Maybe you'll get life, they said
But in my mind it's a sentence of death
While I have no deep wish to die
I'm convinced they'll eventually take my life

Eventually the truth will come to light
Everything will be clear in the daylight
All I've got is what it will take
To resist the system taking my life away

This is what everyone missed as far as news
I was falsely and maliciously accused
Under coercion and outright threats
They left me no choice but to confess

So I gave them only what they wanted
Knowing that I would be taunted
Never thinking it would go this far
As being imprisoned, emotionally scarred

My friends and foes are suddenly alike
Leaving me no chance to fight
Innocent until proven guilty is a farce
They framed me right from the start

Even before my first interview
They swore they already knew the truth
They cut through me just like a knife
Piece by piece, destroying my life

The death penalty is what they said
I hang on to my faith by a thread
In hopes that a miracle can turn back time
Before an innocent man is set to die

Rejected Love

I love you like a brother
Those are the words he heard
The statement cut right through him
Beyond the description of any words

Maybe one day she'll realize
That his love for her is true
He loves her much more than a sister
More than friendship or even family too

She was going to show him
Something she wrote about another man
But she didn't want to hurt him
Even though the pain had already sunk in

Why can't someone hear his cries?
His screams of pain and anguish?
Right now he just wants to die
To melt, to be vanquished

She doesn't love him
That, he now plainly sees
He only wants what's best for her
Even if she doesn't see him

His friends were of no help
They brought him no comfort at all
They didn't see he wasn't himself

Or that he'd taken a nasty fall

He wishes he could fly away
And flee into the dead of night
To run away and hide
It's well within his right

But where will he go?
He has nowhere to turn
No one is around to hear him cry
No one knows how much his heart hurts

His heart yearns for her
He felt that way for no other
But she doesn't love him that way
She loves him like her brother

He's confused and doesn't know what to do
But maybe someday, just maybe somehow
She'll open her eyes
And see what's right in front of her

Maybe one day she'll love him too
Until then he'll keep dreaming
Until he wakes up and finds out
That all of his dreams have come true

Dear New Penpal

Even though we've only written a few times
You have still had a great impact on my life
I was abandoned by friends I thought were true
So it was a blessing to find friendship in you

As our stories will continue to unfold
There are many famous authors I could quote
But I wanted the words to be my own
As seeds of friendship have been sown

Sometimes life is tragic and unfair
But it helps knowing you're somewhere out there
Let me also remind you that there's always hope
And friends who will help us cope

We've both recently been through a lot
And though we don't always agree on every thought
I'm still thankful that to each other we can write
And that in you I've been able to confide

I know that your life has gotten tough
That things have gotten extremely rough
My wish is that I could help you through it
But for now please enjoy this poem as a gift

Remember how you've always remained strong
Through everything that has gone wrong
You share with me what little you've got

And that truly means a lot

Don't take for granted the time you spend
With your family and friends
Use the time wisely and be fair
Because one day they might not be there

Just know that I'm grateful that I met you
And your kindness after everyone else fell through
As my poem now comes to an end
I just want to say thank you for being my friend

Holiday Lost

The New Moon has passed on by
It came as a shock to me
That it was a normal evening in my eyes
Having lost it's usual special meaning

As the holy month of Ramadan now begins
I struggle hard daily to find
The magic of it all again
Because of this illness that's trapped me inside

Most of the magic has been lost
It's tragic to have to say
But that's part of the cost
Of being sick during a holiday

Battle of Angels

Ever since my world was torn
Through life I go on feeling worn
Sadness, grief, despair and pain
All pass through me like a runaway train

I live in a world of violence and death
Always reminding me of what I regret
But with every negative thought I defeat
Others appear and force me to retreat

Surrounded by shadows I hold on to my rope
As best I can, desperately clinging on to hope
But the hope I have comes with light
God has sent the angels to help me fight

No demon will vanquish my mind or my heart
Even though victory and I may seem far apart
My faith in God will show itself in every deed
So in the end I can win and rest in eternal glory

No matter how many times the enemy comes back
The angels will help me counter the attacks
While I don't pray for it to be easy or to not feel pain
I do pray, God please give me the strength

The Fight

They say that change is good
But I fear they might be wrong
The changes I'm seeing in you
Don't seem good at all

You might've stumbled and fell
But that's in the past
Stumbling is part of being human
Haven't we all done that?

These people are trying to destroy you
By sending you on this guilt trip
They tried the same thing with me
Apparently they haven't learned their lesson

Remember than you're not alone
Even if it seems you don't have anyone
God and the angels are with you
I'm even in this fight too

Their manipulations of you are doomed to fail
They tried the same on me, but to no avail
They're not your friends, but your enemies
So listen to me, just for now, please

They're trying to get to me by getting to you
But I'm telling you, they don't have a clue
One day they'll find out that I was right

It'll be something nobody can deny

Our friendship is strong enough to get us through
I will fight with you and for you
On that you can safely bet
Their vile plans, these people will regret

Dear Mom

I wrote this poem just for you
So you wouldn't be left out
The only thing I had to do
Was decide what it was to be about

Even though your name is Ginette
You're known to me as Mom
I want you to know that you're the best
But I think you've known all along

You did everything you could to teach me right
Even when the lessons seemed unfair
In the end I think I turned out alright
You did an awesome job, I swear

If I could write you a song I would
But I don't have the talent to compose
It certainly wouldn't sound as it should
But I can sure do something with prose

This poem is merely a little gift
Filled with things I want you to know
My spirits, you always know how to uplift
Even if sometimes I don't let it show

Before more time has come and gone
I wanted something special for my mom
I'll never be able to adequately thank you for

This day and all the ones that came before

Many things along the way may have gone wrong
But I could count on you to not let me down
You know exactly how strong I can be
Because of you, my mother who deeply loves me

Whether our time left is short or long
There's one last thing I want to say
I love you Mom
More and more every day

Pardon Haiku

Though I pardon you
I'll always hate what you did
Don't do it again

Some People

Some people you love
Some people you don't
Some people you miss
Some people you won't

I'm so happy you're no longer in my life
To the point I don't even notice you're gone
You can no longer contaminate
Everything that I hold dear

Meeting you was the regret of my life
But I don't wish to go back in time
Good people now surround me
And as they say

Some people you love
Some people you don't
Some people you miss
Some people you won't

I have many good things to look forward to
Out here in the free world, unlike you
After this poem I'll think of you no more
You're dead to me even if you're still alive

So today I'm letting everything go
Whether you live well or you perish
Either way, I no longer care

Go ahead and do whatever you want because

Some people you love
Some people you won't
Some people you miss
Some people you don't

A Poem To Duane

I've wracked my brain a thousand ways
To find a way to tell you just how much I hate you
These words might be unbecoming of me
But I have no more fucks left to give, you see
So whatever will be shall just be

I'm the one who held on until the end
But you preferred your selfish ways over your friend
For once I'll really be the bad guy in this story
After all I had to find a way to make my money back
Motherfucker, you're done taking advantage of me

I took the place of your good-for-nothing family
Or at least that's how you described them to me
Not that I still believe any word
That comes out of that lying mouth of yours
And don't think I don't know what you've been up to

You and that wench that talked behind your back
I stood up to her in defence of your ass
But for some reason you picked her over me
You're really fucking stupid if you believe
She won't do to you the same thing she did to me

In that case you two deserve each other
And the misery she'll inevitably bring to your life
You deserve every bad thing that you get
For all the times you talked down to me

And all the times you stabbed me in the back

I feel stupid for putting up with you for so long
For trying everything in the book for us to stay strong
That time you wanted to tie a rope around your neck
I should've told you to burn in hell
To put us both out of the misery you brought to me

Damn me for believing everything you fed to me
Believing you were actually the victim in your own story
When you're the one who took advantage of a little girl
You're exactly where you belong
And you're getting exactly what you deserve

You don't deserve another chance to be free
Now I see you for the predator you really are
And damn me for ever believing otherwise
All this time the truth was right under my nose
But I guess it's better late than never

I gave you endless opportunities to make things right
No matter how sick I was of being labeled the bad guy
But you made your choice, now feel the hurt
You and that wench deserve each other
I'll never be able to forgive you for what you did to me

Unlike others who passed by and did me wrong
I don't wish you well wherever you may go
I hope you live with regret for the rest of you life
While I go on and enjoy what's left of mine
Far away from the bullshit you brought to it for years

I don't know any words in this universe
That capture the animosity left over from your passage
So I leave you these cheap words in memory
Of everything you lost
But I'll never be as cheap to you as you were to me

This is a reminder that your dreams will never come true
And that I'm never gonna be around to help you
Keep forwarding that wench our old letters
Maybe she too will finally see you for what you are
But remember that I'll aways be ten steps ahead

I won't forget to gloat over my own success
When I see you sinking lower and lower
You know it's fitting for the rat you are
You know I could go on and on
But the eight years you took were already too long

I find myself being surprised
Sitting here still showing you mercy
With these words that were supposed to cut you
I'm not being nearly as nasty as I should be
So once again, damn me

I always look forward to the day
Where everything you sent to me is thrown away
No matter where I look I find more of your shit
Just goes to show how deep into my life you got
But know that I'm much happier now that you're not

I'm tired of you so I'll leave things here

But I'm not finished, don't you fear
There's still plenty to be done
I hope you curse the day you were born
Hell hath no fury like a woman scorned

About the Author

Mila Mikhail is an award-winning author based out of Ottawa, Canada's national capital city. In 2018 they were one of the people who received the title of Top Writer on Quora and in 2022 their article "[Forever chemicals are the hidden environmental threat that's already in your blood](#)" was published in the Ottawa Citizen. While not busy with classes at the University of Ottawa, Mila loves cuddling up with their two cats and watching a movie starring Ralph Fiennes.

Visit www.jamilamikhail.com for more information, to get in touch and to download free ebooks.

If you liked this book please give it a good review and consider having a look at Innermost, another collection of poems available in ebook, audiobook and paperback.

Innermost is a collection of both free verse and fixed verse poetry written over a period of half a decade about every emotion felt inside the human heart. These poems will transport you to a whole other world within the innermost depths of the human soul.

www.jamilamikhail.com

www.ingramcontent.com/pod-product-compliance
Lightning Source LLC
Chambersburg PA
CBHW070606050426
42450CB00011B/3003